D0966167

THE
NEW DEAL

Essential Events

THE
NEW DEAL

BY SUSAN E. HAMEN

Content Consultant
Ronald L. Heinemann, professor of history
Hampden-Sydney College

ABDO
Publishing Company

CREDITS

Published by ABDO Publishing Company, 8000 West 78th Street, Edina, Minnesota 55439. Copyright © 2011 by Abdo Consulting Group, Inc. International copyrights reserved in all countries. No part of this book may be reproduced in any form without written permission from the publisher. The Essential Library™ is a trademark and logo of ABDO Publishing Company.

Printed in the United States of America,
North Mankato, Minnesota
062010
092010

 THIS BOOK CONTAINS AT LEAST 10% RECYCLED MATERIALS.

Editor: Rebecca Rowell
Copy Editor: Susan M. Freese
Interior Design and Production: Emily Love
Cover Design: Emily Love

Library of Congress Cataloging-in-Publication Data
Hamen, Susan E.
  The New Deal / Susan E. Hamen.
    p. cm. — (Essential events)
  Includes bibliographical references and index.
  ISBN 978-1-61613-684-0
  1. New Deal, 1933-1939—Juvenile literature. 2.
Depressions—1929—United States—Juvenile literature. 3. United
States—History—1919-1933—Juvenile literature. 4. United States—
History—1933-1945—Juvenile literature. I. Title.
  E806.H296 2011
  973.917—dc22
                                    2010013428

The New Deal

TABLE OF CONTENTS

Chief Justice Charles Evans Hughes swears in Franklin Delano Roosevelt as president of the United States on March 4, 1933.

A New President

Saturday, March 4, 1933, was a cold and dreary day in Washington DC. Despite the bad weather, more than 100,000 Americans gathered at the U.S. Capitol to watch the inauguration of Franklin Delano Roosevelt. He was being sworn in as the thirty-second president of the United States. Millions more people listened in their homes to a radio broadcast of the event. They were desperate to hear if the new president would offer words of hope. The gloomy weather reflected the state of the nation.

As Roosevelt stood on the steps of the Capitol Building and was sworn in by Supreme Court Chief Justice Charles Evans Hughes, he knew his job as president would be a daunting one. Countless Americans were jobless, homeless, and starving. They were looking to him to lead them out of one of the darkest, stormiest periods in U.S. history. Americans were eager to learn if the "New Deal" Roosevelt had mentioned while campaigning would actually do what it promised and pull the nation out of the Great Depression.

By the time Roosevelt took office, the United States was deep into the worst economic depression it had ever experienced. The stock market

The Twentieth Amendment

When Roosevelt won the presidential election, he had to wait nearly four months before being inaugurated on March 4, 1933. The year Roosevelt took office, the Twentieth Amendment was ratified to change inauguration day to January 20 for future presidents.

crash in 1929 had sent the already failing economy further into crisis. Now, four years later, Americans were suffering from the highest unemployment rate in the century. One-quarter of the country was out of work, and many people who were employed held jobs that did not pay enough to support themselves, much less their families. The situation worsened when thousands of Americans lost their homes and farms. Many found themselves living on the streets or in makeshift shacks with other homeless people.

Ready for Change

The nation was in despair, and no end to the crisis seemed in sight. People had lost faith in their government and in President Herbert Hoover, Roosevelt's predecessor. Hoover had assured the country, "We have passed the worst."[1] But this proved untrue, and Americans were ready for change.

As the poverty level rose, Americans began to blame Hoover for not doing more to stop the crisis.

Hoover Hogs

In the South, some people were so poor and hungry during the Depression they caught and ate jack-rabbits. Some people in Texas ate armadillos. The animals were often referred to as "Hoover hogs" or "poverty pigs."

Families that had been evicted from their homes huddled together in shantytowns on the edges of cities, living in shacks built of scrap metal, wooden crates, and tar paper. These crude camp settlements were called "Hoovervilles" after the president, the person the homeless blamed for their calamity.

FRANKLIN DELANO ROOSEVELT

The man who would inherit this crisis was Franklin Delano Roosevelt. The president's background was very different from many of the poverty-stricken people who had voted him into office. Roosevelt was born on January 30, 1882, into a wealthy family that lived in

The Bonus Army

In 1924, the U.S. Congress passed a law providing millions of World War I veterans with insurance policies that could be redeemed for their cash value in 1945. But these men were struggling to survive during the Great Depression, and they demanded the money, called a bonus, be paid immediately.

After being denied, the veterans decided to protest. This Bonus Army, as it was called, met in Washington DC in spring 1932. More than 15,000 veterans from across the country, many with their wives and children, camped along the Anacostia River.

On June 15, the U.S. House of Representatives passed an act that would allow the Bonus Army veterans to collect their money. But the Senate did not approve the legislation. As the protestors grew more upset, Hoover feared a revolt. He ordered the Bonus Army removed from the city. On July 28, General Douglas MacArthur and hundreds of U.S. Army soldiers used tanks, bayonets, and tear gas to drive out the protestors. The scene of these once-honored heroes being forced to retreat by fellow soldiers was shocking to Americans.

The "Pay the Bonus" sign carried by this group of World War I veterans was typical of the banners throughout the demonstration by the Bonus Army in Washington DC in 1932.

Hyde Park, New York. His father, James Roosevelt, was a railroad and coal executive. His mother, Sara Delano Roosevelt, was from an influential family.

Roosevelt was raised with the advantages of wealth, but his parents taught him to have a sense of discipline and moral responsibility. He graduated from Harvard University, where he served as editor of the university newspaper. Roosevelt attended Columbia University Law School and passed the bar examination without graduating.

Roosevelt worked in a New York City law firm as a clerk for three years. In 1910, at the age of 28, he ran for the New York State Senate as a Democrat and won.

In 1913, President Woodrow Wilson appointed Roosevelt to the position of assistant secretary of the navy. Living in Washington DC for seven years, he learned much about politics. During World War I, Roosevelt worked on wartime projects that earned him the reputation as a man who could get things done. In 1920, he ran as the vice presidential candidate on the Democratic ticket, which lost in a Republican landslide.

Roosevelt was elected governor of New York in 1928 and soon thereafter was forced to deal with problems created by the Depression. He succeeded in creating aid programs and tax relief for many struggling families in his state. His aggressive approach to securing aid for New Yorkers helped him get nominated as the Democratic candidate for president in 1932. He and John Nance Garner would run

Why Roosevelt Wanted to Be President

A *New York Times* reporter wrote about Roosevelt becoming president: "When I asked him once, before his nomination, why he wanted to be President in a time like this, he answered, smiling, that some one had to be, some one with no more than human capacity, to meet a crisis that eventually would have to be resolved by human intelligence. The answer was made lightly. . . . But even then I saw it was not meant lightly."[2]

against the incumbent Republican president, Herbert Hoover.

Roosevelt accepted his party's nomination and promised his supporters, "I pledge you, I pledge myself, to a new deal for the American people."[3] Although it was not yet clear to Americans what this new deal entailed, they knew they had a choice. Voters could reelect a president who seemed unable to end the Great Depression, or they could elect a man who promised aid, a balanced budget, and more jobs.

In November 1932, U.S. voters made it clear they were ready for change. Roosevelt won the election in a landslide victory, and Democrats won control of Congress. The nation now looked to Roosevelt and the Democratic Party for relief and hope. ⌐

Letters to the New President

Americans' reactions to Franklin D. Roosevelt's inaugural address were immediate. During the first week of his presidency, the White House was inundated with stacks of letters and telegrams—a few hundred thousand—from desperate Americans.

Franklin D. Roosevelt entered the Oval Office ready to take on the challenges brought by the Great Depression.

Henry Ford's Model T changed the lives of many Americans.

THE ROARING TWENTIES

The pain of the Great Depression was in marked contrast to the frivolity of the previous decade. The end of World War I in 1918 made way for a promising future. Americans were eager to forget the war and return to normal life.

By the 1920s, Americans were enjoying a time of economic prosperity, increased income, and more liberal lifestyles. A new, modern age developed, brought about by social and cultural changes. Young people began wearing less restrictive clothing, and ladies dared to cut their hair to short lengths and wear cosmetics. Women also began to smoke and drink like men did, which in the past had been considered inappropriate. The glitz and glamour of the nation's first movie stars and sports heroes, such as Rudolph Valentino and Babe Ruth, drew the attention of wealthy and poor alike. The decade's greatest hero was Charles Lindbergh, who in 1927 became the first person to fly across the Atlantic Ocean solo. Jazz music provided yet another exhilarating experience, and the era was coined the Jazz Age.

The 1920s were a time of great change and hope in the United States. As the stock market rose steadily, boosting people's confidence

The Jazz Age

The 1920s are often referred to as the Jazz Age. Musicians such as Count Basie, Duke Ellington, and Paul Whiteman helped popularize the style of music called jazz. Throughout the 1920s and 1930s, jazz advanced to become a sophisticated form of music that included improvisation, or free and spontaneous performance. Radio stations featured live performances by jazz bands. Louis Armstrong, a popular jazz musician of the time, was believed by many to be the world's best trumpet player.

in the U.S. economy, the national income rose 40 percent between 1922 and 1929. And the booming economy and rising wages allowed more and more families to afford more than mere necessities. The consumer culture had arrived. By 1927, two-thirds of U.S. homes had been wired for electricity, the newest life-changing technology. The introduction of household appliances such as the washing machine, refrigerator, toaster, and vacuum cleaner allowed daily chores to be done much more easily. Such inventions drastically reduced the amount of time needed to perform household tasks.

The development of the radio provided a remarkable new line of communication and entertainment for people. Radio sales during this time, known also as the Roaring Twenties, jumped from $60 million in 1922 to nearly $850 million in 1929. Life was improving for the majority of Americans, who could not imagine the dark days that lay ahead.

A New Form of Freedom

During this time, Henry Ford's Model T automobile forever changed the course of history. He had been developing his version of the automobile since the late 1800s. Ford's revolutionary and efficient assembly line process, along with stiff competition from other automobile manufacturers, allowed him to sell the Model T for only $290 in 1927. Previously, only the wealthy could afford such a luxury, but this price was affordable for most U.S. families.

Having an automobile meant freedom and mobility. People moved from the inner cities to the suburbs. Taking a family vacation to a far-off seaside resort or a mountain lodge became possible for many people.

A New Era

The 1920s was an era of change. The United States had moved from the war-time era of the Great War, or World War I (1914–1918), to one of peace and prosperity. It was a decade in which new technology, new music, new styles, and new attitudes emerged. Women in particular experienced great change during this decade. After years of fighting for support from citizens and politicians alike, women won the right to vote when the Nineteenth Amendment was ratified in 1920. As voters, women achieved greater equality, and they began to challenge society's standards.

This behavior was also true of the young. Many younger Americans were eager to pursue fun and adventurous lifestyles. Their desire for change was reflected in literature, music, art, fashion, and architecture, all of which became more expressive and spirited than they had ever been. The era has been referred to by many names, including the Roaring Twenties, the Age of Intolerance, the Age of Wonderful Nonsense, and the Jazz Age. Regardless of the name, the culture and styles of the decade were new and distinct, and many people still treasure them today.

Young people escaped the watchful eyes of their parents. And the oil and rubber and road-building industries were revolutionized.

A Booming Stock Market

While the nation enjoyed a booming economy, stock market prices continued to climb to unbelievable levels. People invested large sums of money in stocks, and the money went to the companies in which people invested.

A stock is a share, or piece, of a publicly held company, which is owned by a group of shareholders rather than by a person or a small group of people. Stocks are bought and sold on the stock market by investors. When a publicly held company does well and makes a profit, its shareholders receive part of this profit in the form of a dividend. When a publicly held company does not do well, its shareholders lose money. The more shares a person owns, the more money he or she can make or lose.

At times, the value of a company's stock can be inflated, or more than its true worth. For instance, if many people wish to invest in one company because they believe it will be successful and pay large dividends, the demand for this stock will drive up its price. In some cases, the price of the stock may be greater than its true value.

In the 1920s, ordinary people began playing the stock market with their hard-earned savings or newly available credit. They bought on margin, putting up only a part of the price. This practice of buying and selling stock in the hope of making a quick profit is called speculating. As more and more people speculated in the stock market, prices climbed to remarkable highs.

THE STOCK MARKET CRASHES

The boom in the stock market, dependent on credit and an ever-expanding economy, would not last forever. By the late 1920s, U.S. businesses were producing goods faster than consumers could afford to buy them. Supply was greater than demand. In September and October 1929, the stock market experienced

The Great Gatsby

The Great Gatsby, a novel written by F. Scott Fitzgerald and published in 1925, is a detailed portrait of the decade. The story centers on Jay Gatsby, a poor Midwesterner who moved to New York City and became extremely wealthy selling liquor illegally. He becomes famous for throwing lavish parties in his mansion on Long Island, New York. One of the main themes of the book is the decline in moral standards during the 1920s. In 2005, *Time* magazine ranked *The Great Gatsby* as one of the top 100 best novels of all time.

Crowds panic in the Wall Street district of Manhattan in New York City on October 24, 1929.

some downturns. Nervous shareholders began selling their stocks, which drove stock prices down even further.

On October 24, 1929, "Black Thursday," the stock market crashed. Stocks steadied on Friday and Saturday, but by Monday, prices were dropping again. On "Black Tuesday," October 29, a panic by shareholders led to record sales of 16,410,030 shares. Prices plummeted nearly 80 percent. Investors lost huge sums of money.

THE GREAT DEPRESSION BEGINS

The collapse of the stock market was only one of many economic factors that caused and worsened the Great Depression. Industrial production had exceeded demand. Consumers who lost money in the market crash had exhausted their credit lines. Others had low-paying jobs and could not buy cars and homes. Unsold inventories led companies to lay off workers.

Farmers experienced a decline in crop prices, which reduced their purchasing power. Furthermore, many farmers were unable to repay their loans and mortgages to local banks. Foreclosed farms and farm machinery were sold for just pennies on the dollar, causing banks to lose more money. Soon, hundreds of banks, which had been inadequately regulated, were forced out of business.

High taxes on foreign goods restricted trade. Europeans purchased fewer U.S. goods, and

"The most disastrous decline in the biggest and broadest stock market of history rocked the financial district yesterday. In the very midst of the collapse five of the country's most influential bankers hurried to the office of J. P. Morgan & Co., and after a brief conference gave out word that they believe the foundations of the market to be sound, that the market smash has been caused by technical rather than fundamental considerations, and that many sound stocks are selling too low."[1]

—New York Times,
October 25, 1929

Speakeasies

In 1919, the Eighteenth Amendment was ratified. It went into effect in 1920. The amendment established prohibition, which made the manufacture, transportation, and sale of alcoholic beverages illegal. Alcohol consumption dropped sharply after passage of this amendment, but many Americans ignored the ban and got alcohol from people called bootleggers, who provided liquor to consumers. Much of this traffic was taken over by gangsters, the most notorious of whom was Al Capone. People drank in secret, illegal bars called speakeasies. The Eighteenth Amendment was repealed by the Twenty-first Amendment in 1933, which made drinking legal again.

European governments defaulted on their debts to the United States from World War I. The financial depression would spread to the rest of the world.

The Federal Reserve Board, which oversees the U.S. banking system, had pursued easy credit policies in the 1920s that fueled market speculation. The board tightened credit in the aftermath of the crash. This left the banks in need of cash and reduced their capacity to loan money. The supply of money lessened, and the economy could not recover.

Following the October 1929 stock market crash, the U.S. economy slumped nearly every month until 1933. The United States was in the middle of the Great Depression, and no hope seemed in sight. Confidence in the economic system was shattered. Gone were the days of the carefree Roaring Twenties.

A former millionaire sells apples on a street corner in California. He lost his fortune and his job as a result of the stock market crash in 1929.

Franklin D. Roosevelt called a special session of Congress on March 9, 1933, to deal with the banking crisis.

ROOSEVELT TAKES ACTION

When Franklin D. Roosevelt became president of the United States, he knew he had to take immediate action. The nation was in a state of disaster. Millions of people had lost all their savings when thousands of the nation's banks locked their doors and went out of business. Many of the Americans who still held jobs were earning only a portion of what they had once brought home, making it almost impossible to meet basic needs. As factories reduced the workweek to only a few days, salaries and wages were slashed.

DESPERATION

By 1933, nearly 15 million Americans were unemployed. This meant that one in four workers was without a job. Men who had once held jobs as bankers, accountants, and business owners found themselves selling fruit and newspapers on street corners. To come up with money for food and rent, families sold their cars, furniture, and other possessions until they had nothing left to sell. Wives mended tattered clothing, and children wore ill-fitting hand-me-downs. Having new shoes became a luxury few could afford. Author Nick Taylor described the scene in

Younger Victims

In addition to the many children who, along with their parents, were homeless during the Great Depression, a large number were abandoned—as many as 400,000 in October 1932. During this time, approximately 200,000 children became hobos, traveling the country in search of jobs and necessities, including food and shelter. Others lived in groups and scavenged and begged for food.

Hobos

Many of the more than 2 million homeless Americans in the 1930s were men and boys who became hobos. They illegally hopped railroad freight cars and traveled hundreds of miles in search of work. Riding the rails was dangerous. To hop a train, a hobo would grab hold of and then jump into an open boxcar as the train began to move. Many hobos fell from the train and lost limbs or were killed. Even those who made it on board the car faced danger. The railroads hired guards to keep hobos off trains, and they usually used brute force to do so.

American–Made: The Enduring Legacy of the WPA: When FDR Put the Nation to Work:

Factories lay idle, storefronts vacant, fields plowed under. State governments, cities, and towns had exhausted their meager relief funds. The desolation knew no boundaries: the skilled and the unskilled alike stood in the breadlines, waited their turns in soup kitchens, scavenged in town dumps; when they were evicted from their homes they built impromptu shacks to house their families until the police came and knocked the shantytowns down.[1]

Soup kitchens were usually run by churches and other charitable organizations, and they served up to three meals a day to those unable to afford food. Hunger had become an unpleasant reality for many Americans, including children.

The Dust Bowl

Struggling farmers had to face another setback as well. Years of farming in the Great Plains states had

A gigantic dust cloud overtakes a ranch in Boise City, Oklahoma, in 1935. This was a common scene in the Dust Bowl.

created poor soil conditions and a lack of natural vegetation. Farmers had planted the same crops year after year, which left an imbalance of nutrients in the earth. Ranchers had allowed cattle to overgraze, further damaging the topsoil and reducing the area of vegetation necessary to prevent erosion.

A woman attempts to clean after a dust storm.

When a great drought hit the Great Plains during the 1930s, the dry topsoil was blown away by severe dust storms. Millions of tons of black dirt were picked up by the high winds and blown as far as the East Coast. These dust storms, known as "black blizzards," left homes and farms covered in dust. Even though people sealed their doors and windows, nearly everything became covered with dust by the high-speed winds. People who were caught outside during a storm could barely see their hands in front of their faces. The filthy air also caused dust pneumonia, a lung disease that made it difficult for people to breathe even while indoors.

Colorado, Kansas, New Mexico, Oklahoma, and Texas were hit hardest by the dust storms, and the region soon became a dry, dusty land. This area of approximately 50 million acres (20 million ha) became known as the Dust Bowl. Without the topsoil that had blown away, the area became unable to grow crops. One-quarter of Dust Bowl farm families packed up whatever belongings they could transport and headed to California and Oregon. They had heard rumors that the fruit and vegetable growers in these states were hiring all who applied.

"People tried to protect themselves by hanging wet sheets in front of doorways and windows to filter the dirt. They stuffed window frames with gummed tape and rags. But keeping the fine particles out was impossible. The dust permeated the tiniest cracks and crevices. Through it all, the farmers kept plowing, kept sowing wheat, kept waiting for rain."[2]

—Surviving the Dust Bowl, *a film broadcast on PBS's* American Experience

Immediate Action

Roosevelt knew millions of people were counting on him to lead the country out of the dark days of the Great Depression. When he gave his inaugural address, Roosevelt addressed the horrific situation Americans were experiencing:

> I am certain that my fellow Americans expect that on my induction into the Presidency I will address them with a candor and a decision which the present situation of our Nation impels. This is preeminently the time to speak the truth, the whole truth, frankly and boldly. Nor need we shrink from honestly facing conditions in our country today. This great Nation will endure as it has endured, will revive and will prosper. So, first of all, let me assert my firm belief that the only thing we have to fear is fear itself—nameless, unreasoning, unjustified terror which paralyzes needed efforts to convert retreat into advance.[3]

Once he was inaugurated, Roosevelt took action. With banks failing nationwide, he proclaimed a national bank holiday. He was attempting to avert further financial panic. Effective March 6, 1933, all banks would be closed, ensuring that people could not rush to their bank and demand any money they had deposited. Such bank runs, as they were called, forced banks to close their doors when they ran out of cash to meet customers' withdrawals. For the few days banks were closed, Americans would have to make do with the cash they had on hand.

During the bank holiday, on Thursday, March 9, the U.S. Congress met in special session and passed the Emergency Banking Act. The first measure in the New Deal, the bill strictly regulated banks and gave the U.S. Treasury power to issue more currency. The most important feature of the Emergency Banking Act allowed government accountants to inspect banks' records before they reopened.

On Monday, March 13, banks reopened. Citizens responded favorably by

Eleanor Roosevelt

Eleanor Roosevelt was not a glamorous woman, but she was a heroine to many Americans, fighting for human rights during the country's darkest days. Earlier in her life Eleanor had had little self-confidence. As a child, Eleanor was often told by family members that she was unattractive.

In 1903, as a teenager, Eleanor began to volunteer at a house for immigrants in New York. She brought along her distant relative Franklin and introduced him to the difficult world of the poor. That year, the two became engaged. They married in 1905. Eleanor's uncle, President Theodore Roosevelt, gave her away at the wedding.

When Franklin became president, he wanted Eleanor to stop volunteering and focus on being the White House hostess as First Lady. Eleanor convinced him to allow her to travel the country to learn what was going on. Eleanor described to Franklin the suffering of impoverished Americans nationwide.

One of Eleanor's primary concerns was racial discrimination. She tried to get Congress to pass an antilynching bill. Although she was unsuccessful and upset some people with her activism, Eleanor gained an enormous amount of respect and admiration from many Americans for her efforts.

depositing more of their money. Roosevelt's swift action proved successful in restoring some of the nation's confidence in its banking system. The bank holiday reassured Americans they were not alone but in the situation together. Many, although inconvenienced, were relieved that something was finally being done to help the crisis.

Roosevelt's Emergency Banking Act was the first of many bills passed and programs created to battle the nation's disastrous economic situation. Roosevelt's days were filled with making speeches, holding press conferences, meeting with his cabinet, and talking with advisors.

Roosevelt's first months in office are referred to as his "first 100 days." Never before in U.S. history had so much legislative action taken place so quickly. Fifteen emergency acts were passed in this very short time. This and subsequent legislation came to be known as the New Deal.

Roosevelt spent his first 100 days as president
signing numerous bills into law.

President Roosevelt delivered his first radio "fireside chat" in March 1933.

THE NEW DEAL

*P*resident Roosevelt's New Deal was a
hodgepodge of economic and social
legislation created to address the problems brought
on by the Depression. Roosevelt was willing to try
almost anything to revive the economy. In a speech

in Atlanta, Georgia, during his campaign for president, he had said, "The country demands bold, persistent experimentation. It is common sense to take a method and try it: if it fails, admit it frankly and try another. But above all, try something."[1] This was the approach Roosevelt took as he guided the United States to recovery from the Depression.

FIRESIDE CHATS

On March 12, 1933, Roosevelt began speaking to Americans in radio programs he called "fireside chats." He would ultimately give 27 of these chats, speaking directly to the people in their homes. During his first fireside chat, Roosevelt reassured Americans that it was safe to keep their money in the reopened banks. In simple terms, he explained the steps the government was taking to guarantee this. His calm, soothing voice assured millions of listeners they were all in this difficult time together, and that united, they would make it through.

Roosevelt had a great sense of empathy—the ability to understand

"You people must have faith; you must not be stampeded by rumors or guesses. Let us unite in banishing fear. We have provided the machinery to restore our financial system, and it is up to you to support and make it work. It is your problem, my friends, no less than it is mine. Together we cannot fail."[2]

—*Franklin D. Roosevelt,*
first fireside chat,
March 12, 1933

the needs and motives of other people. His struggle with polio may have cultivated this quality.

In August 1921, while vacationing with his family, Roosevelt was struck with polio. The disease partially paralyzed his legs, arms, hands, and back. He would eventually regain the use of his arms, hands, and back, but at the age of 39, Roosevelt lost full use of his legs.

Roosevelt spent time each day in physical therapy trying to regain the ability to walk. Eventually, with leg braces and crutches, he was able to walk with support from another person. His experience gave

Polio

Between 1915 and 1945, at least 1,500 cases of polio were reported annually in the United States. In 1916, a staggering 27,363 people were diagnosed with the virus, which attacks nerve cells in the brain and the spinal cord. Patients who have a mild reaction to the virus get a fever, headache, and sore throat that last only a day or so. A severe attack results in a stiff neck and back. Muscles weaken, and sufferers may have pain in their legs and back, and they may become paralyzed.

Bulbar paralysis, the most serious form of polio, results in nerve damage in the brain stem. Patients can lose muscle control in their eyes, tongue, face, and neck, making them unable to swallow and breathe.

Patients who needed help to breathe were placed in a ventilator known as an "iron lung." This chamber changed air pressure to force air in and out of the patient's lungs. Many patients spent years confined, lying down in an iron lung. In May 2009, a woman named Martha Mason died after 60 years in an iron lung.

In 1955, Jonas E. Salk's vaccine against polio was approved for use. Today, polio has been nearly wiped out in developed countries such as the United States.

him the determination to fight overwhelming odds to pull his nation out of the Great Depression.

CREATING JOBS

With the nation's banking system on the mend, Roosevelt and his administration focused on the general state of the economy. After the banks reopened, Congress passed its second piece of legislation. The Economy Act cut government spending to balance the federal budget. The act ultimately reorganized government agencies, reduced benefit payments to veterans, and cut federal employees' salaries by 15 percent.

Roosevelt believed creating jobs was critical. Getting people back to work would put money in their pockets. In turn, they would be able to buy food, clothing, and other basic goods. This new spending would boost sales and put factories and manufacturers back in operation.

On March 31, 1933, Roosevelt created the Civilian Conservation

Warm Springs

Franklin D. Roosevelt started a center for polio patients in Warm Springs, Georgia. He had spent several months each year at Warm Springs, swimming in the warm mineral water, which helped lessen the effects of his polio. There, he met several other people with polio, many of whom had a hard time affording treatment. Roosevelt purchased the land in 1926 and established the Georgia Warm Springs Foundation the following year to provide low-cost treatment to victims of polio.

Members of the CCC clear trees in George Washington National Park in Virginia in April 1933 to make their camp site.

Corps (CCC). Several federal departments—Agriculture, Labor, War, and Interior—worked together to create a program that would put young men to work on a variety of outdoor projects, including improving national parks and strengthening flood control. By August, approximately 300,000 young men had been transported to camps to live and receive training.

The CCC was administered by the U.S. Army. Only unemployed and unmarried men ages 18 to 25 and from families receiving relief from the government were hired. They received $30 a month,

$25 of which had to be sent home to their families. The workers lived in barracks and ate in mess halls, just as soldiers did.

Working with the forestry service, CCC workers planted more than 2 billion trees, cleared hiking paths, built shelters and fire observation towers, and thinned overgrown forests. At times, they were called on to fight forest fires, blast rock, conduct topographical surveys, and install water lines.

Eventually, almost 3 million men worked as part of the CCC. Their efforts can still be seen in national and state parks across the United States. The CCC is still considered one of the New Deal's most successful and popular programs.

FEDERAL EMERGENCY RELIEF ACT

The Federal Emergency Relief Act (FERA), which became law on May 12, 1933, also provided much-needed relief to the unemployed. Harry Lloyd Hopkins was the administrator of FERA. Hopkins, a social worker, was eager and ready to take immediate action. While debating with one legislator about providing long-range

CCC Enrollment

Within days of the CCC being created, 25,000 men from 16 cities had signed up to work for the program. When the U.S. Forest Service and Park Service opened the program's enrollment to Native Americans, more than 80,000 men from tribes nationwide served.

relief, Hopkins argued, "People don't eat in the long run, Senator. They eat every day."[3]

Hopkins ran his office out of a run-down building, insisting he was not about to waste money on operating costs. Aware of families' immediate needs, Hopkins gave out $5.3 million in relief funds his first day on the job.

FERA gave direct relief such as food, clothing, and shelter. It also sponsored a variety of work relief programs in cooperation with state governments that shared the costs. Millions of Americans built roads, schools, parks, and sewers with FERA money.

Two other early work relief programs were the Public Works Administration (PWA), created on June 16, 1933, and the Civil Works Administration (CWA), created on November 8. The CWA provided federal money to states during the winter of 1933–1934 for small construction projects that would employ workers immediately. The PWA was a long-range program that funded larger construction projects on major roadways, dams, hospitals, sewage treatment plants, bridges, university buildings, and military installations. The Hoover Dam in Nevada and the Overseas Highway linking the Florida Keys were PWA projects.

Harry Lloyd Hopkins

A long line of men wait for a sandwich and a cup of coffee in Times Square, New York City, on February 13, 1932.

GETTING BACK ON TRACK

*G*etting Americans back to work was only part of President Roosevelt's recovery plan. The United States needed much more to recover from the Great Depression. The Roosevelt administration also had to address the farm crisis.

Even before the stock market crashed in October 1929, farmers had been struggling with low crop prices due to a surplus of grain and livestock. The Agricultural Adjustment Act (AAA), which was passed on May 13, 1933, established crop control methods to reduce the surplus.

The AAA dealt with seven farm products: corn, wheat, cotton, rice, hogs, tobacco, and milk. Through the domestic allotment plan, farmers received money for leaving their fields unplanted or for plowing under healthy crops instead of harvesting them. Milk was poured out instead of being sold. To reduce the number of pigs being raised for food, 6 million of the animals were slaughtered in September 1933, and the meat was given to relief organizations such as the Federal Surplus Relief Corporation.

The reduction in supply raised prices. In 1933, 10 million acres (4,046,856 ha) of cotton were plowed under and cotton prices rose from 5.5¢ per pound to 9.9¢. Although many people were

Reducing Crops

Under the AAA, farmers were paid to reduce crop production. In the South, the cotton crop was reduced by 33 percent in 1934. The same year, the tobacco crop was reduced by 30 percent, or 13 million pounds (5,896,701 kg), and the price for the crop doubled. Tobacco farmers were paid $17.50 for each acre of tobacco they did not grow.

angry that food crops were being destroyed during a time when so many people were hungry, farm incomes rose more than $3 billion from 1932 to 1935. Thanks to the AAA, farmers were earning an adequate living for the first time in several years.

HOME FORECLOSURES

At the time of Roosevelt's inauguration, banks were evicting thousands of Americans from their homes. To ease this problem, Congress created the Home Owners' Loan Corporation (HOLC) on June 13, 1933. The HOLC would exchange its bonds for mortgages in difficulty, which protected the banks. The agency then negotiated easier payment terms with the home owner, who would pay the HOLC. The HOLC made more than 1 million loans to home owners, though doing so did not mean that all of these homes were saved.

Going Hungry

While farmers were pouring out milk and plowing under crops, many Americans were starving. While the prices of the era were far lower than they are today, at the time, many people simply could not afford to buy even these most basic foods.

THE TENNESSEE VALLEY AUTHORITY

The Tennessee Valley Authority (TVA) was another program initiated during Roosevelt's first 100 days. Created by the TVA Act on May 18,

1933, the TVA was an independent public corporation created to produce electric power and control flooding along the Tennessee River and its tributaries. The TVA became a successful New Deal program.

During World War I, the federal government had constructed a hydroelectric power plant and two munitions plants on the Tennessee River at Muscle Shoals, Alabama. After years of sitting idle, TVA reactivated the power plant, which used water to create electricity. A series of new dams was constructed that prevented the river from flooding farms and eroding fertile soil over a seven-state area.

Advantages of Farming

Many families lost their farms to the banks during the Great Depression. However, those who were able to keep their farms sometimes had an easier time than those living in cities. As Carmen Carter recalled, "But when we read about the bread lines and soup kitchens in the cities, we felt we were lucky because we raised our own food. Our house was rent free, just keep it in repair. Our fuel, which was wood, was free for the cutting. Then our second child, Iris, was born and our biggest expense was doctor bills. However, this too was solved when our doctor agreed to take turkeys and garden produce for pay."[1]

Privately owned utility companies were not happy about the TVA. They accused the government-run agency of stealing their business. But the power plant provided cheap electricity to the area, making it possible for many residents to afford electricity for the first time. This greatly improved the quality of life for many people living in the rural area.

National Recovery Administration

The National Industrial Recovery Act (NIRA) was a far-reaching plan designed to help industry recover. The NIRA created the National Recovery Administration (NRA) to supervise a cooperative effort between business, labor, and the government to revive the economy. When the NRA was created on June 16, 1933, it gave the federal government more control over U.S. business than ever before. More than 500 codes were designed to impose wage and price controls. These codes were intended to eliminate

---

Escape to the Movies

Although Americans cut their spending drastically during the Depression, 60 to 85 million Americans attended a movie theater once a week. For about a quarter an adult could forget the hard times of everyday life and escape to the charming, colorful world of the movies. To convince more people to attend more movies, theaters offered prizes and cut ticket prices.

Some of the popular movie genres of the time included musicals, gangster films, Westerns, and comedies. In 1937, Walt Disney released his first full-length, color animation movie, *Snow White and the Seven Dwarfs*. In 1939, *The Wizard of Oz* was released, showing Dorothy being swept from the bleak world of Kansas to the magical world of Oz. Released the same year, *Gone with the Wind* was another brilliantly colored film. Set in the South during the Civil War, it reinforced the idea of struggling to overcome terrible odds.

The color movie was a relatively new invention, and audiences were thrilled by its breathtaking images. For the short time they watched a movie, Americans could forget about the difficulties waiting for them in the real world outside theater doors.

destructive competition between businesses. Among other things, businesses that joined the NRA agreed not to reduce prices below certain amounts. That way, they would not compete with each other.

The NRA plan called for creating federally licensed trade associations for each type of business. The leaders of these associations worked with the federal government to decide the amounts of products to be created, the selling prices for such goods, and the wages that workers would receive.

NRA codes also required collective bargaining. In this process, employers negotiate with groups of workers formed into unions rather than with individuals. Negotiations address such issues as wages and working conditions.

The symbol of the NRA was a big blue eagle clutching a cogwheel and lightning bolts in its talons. Businesses that supported the NRA

"NRA did more for the nation's morale than for its pocketbook. It did create a lively and exhilarating sense of moving ahead, of getting something done. Everyone felt . . . that he had a part in it. . . . The NRA also made the people aware . . . that through their government they could strike directly and tellingly at glaring social evils, such as child labor, the sweatshop, the six-day week and the ten-hour day, and the denial of the right to collective bargaining. The NRA moved the country a long step forward in these respects, and there has been no falling back since."[2]

—*Cabell Phillips,*
From the Crash to the Blitz

displayed posters with this symbol. Americans felt a sense of patriotism and duty to support the NRA, and they often boycotted stores that did not sell NRA-member products.

Many business owners, however, opposed the NRA. Members of the NRA were not allowed to manufacture more items than the federal government specified. They were also restricted from selling goods at even a penny lower than the regulated price, even if they could still make a profit by doing so. Many business owners argued that the program interfered with free enterprise and broke antitrust laws, which had been suspended. Labor leaders also complained that wage and hour laws were being violated.

But such criticisms did not stop the Roosevelt administration from creating New Deal programs. The president kept moving ahead with his ideas, doing what he thought was best for the country and its people. He continued to plan for and work toward bringing the nation out of the Depression that had for too long caused Americans to suffer.

The emblem of the National Recovery Administration

President Roosevelt signed the banking bill into law on March 9, 1933.

RELIEF, RECOVERY, AND REFORM

The New Deal was intended to provide immediate help to the nation. Roosevelt's plan has generally been divided into three types of action: relief, recovery, and reform. Relief plans provided immediate aid to the destitute. Recovery efforts were designed to stimulate the economy. Reform programs were intended to bring about permanent changes and improvements.

Roosevelt had gained such strong congressional support that he was able to swiftly pass 15 major bills in his first 100 days in office. This had never been done by any other president.

THE BANKING ACT OF 1933

One of the bills passed during Roosevelt's first 100 days was the Banking Act of 1933. Sections of it are referred to as the Glass-Steagall Banking Act. After establishing regulations for banking, Roosevelt solidified the security of the nation's banks. The Glass-Steagall Act prohibited banks from using customers' savings deposits to invest in the stock market.

The act also created the Federal Deposit Insurance Corporation (FDIC). The FDIC insured money a person deposited in a bank. The U.S. government guaranteed depositors they would receive every penny back, up to $5,000, should the bank fail.

So Many Bills

Will Rogers, a popular humorist of the time, joked of Roosevelt's first 100 days in office, saying, "Congress doesn't pass legislation anymore—they just wave at the bills as they go by."[1]

Sharecroppers Get a Rough Deal

Not all Americans clearly benefited from Roosevelt's various New Deal programs. For instance, Roosevelt's AAA bill was intended to assist farmers by raising prices for crops, but the aid the government gave them did not trickle down to others. Sharecroppers were poor farmers who lived on large farms owned by a landlord. The land owner provided sharecroppers with land, tools, seed, and a house. These farmers worked the land and planted and harvested the crops. They then paid the landlord with a large portion of the money earned from the harvested crops.

Gardening to Survive

Many families relied on gardens for produce. Those who lived in the country also gathered berries and nuts and caught fish to supplement their food supply. Women spent hours over hot woodstoves canning and preserving fruits, vegetables, and meat, which provided food throughout the winter.

The system of sharecropping existed primarily in the South. A high percentage of sharecropper families were black and usually very poor. Children of sharecroppers often worked alongside their parents in the fields as soon as they were big enough to help.

When the AAA paid farmers to produce fewer crops, few landlords shared their payments with their sharecroppers. In fact, some

An African-American sharecropper family in November 1939. The family had little to share for their Thanksgiving meal.

sharecroppers and their families were evicted from the land. Many of these families migrated to cities in search of work. But urban areas were already teeming with unemployed workers in search of jobs. The arrival of these poor farmers simply added to the number of poor Americans trying to survive in cities that had little or no employment opportunities.

The Resettlement Administration

The Resettlement Administration (RA) was established on April 30, 1935, to address the plight of farmers from the South and Southwest, as well as other agricultural workers from the Dust Bowl region. Farmers were given loans to move to areas with fertile soil and favorable weather conditions to begin farming again. Others received money to help them buy necessary equipment or animals for their farms.

The RA also funded special projects to document the hardships of the Great Depression. The Photography Project captured rural poverty through thousands of photographs. As part of this project,

---

Migrant Mother

Photographer Dorothea Lange captured on film the despair experienced by many Americans during the Great Depression. Perhaps the most well-known of Lange's work is "Migrant Mother," a photograph of Florence Owens Thompson and her children. Lange snapped images of the family in Nipomo, California, in early 1936.

More than 20 years after taking the historic images, Lange spoke about the experience in *Popular Photography*:

I saw and approached the hungry and desperate mother, as if drawn by a magnet. I do not remember how I explained my presence or my camera to her, but I do remember she asked me no questions. I made five exposures, working closer and closer from the same direction. I did not ask her name or her history. She told me her age, that she was thirty-two. She said that they had been living on frozen vegetables from the surrounding fields, and birds that the children killed. She had just sold the tires from her car to buy food. There she sat in that lean-to tent with her children huddled around her, and seemed to know that my pictures might help her, and so she helped me. There was a sort of equality about it.[2]

photographer Dorothea Lange took some of the most memorable photographs of the era, especially of migratory farm workers. The RA's Film Project produced documentary films about the Depression. Another RA project sent folklorists nationwide to record and preserve folk music for future generations.

Minorities Endure the Depression

Minorities in the United States had suffered high levels of unemployment and discrimination before the Great Depression. Now,

Eleanor Roosevelt on the Road

Eleanor Roosevelt took an interest in the Resettlement Administration (RA). Driving her own car, she traveled around to see for herself the poor conditions Americans lived in. While the trips did not please the members of the Secret Service assigned to watch over and protect the First Lady, her trips were helpful to her husband and many Americans. She reported her findings to the president. The RA helped move many of the families Mrs. Roosevelt saw into better housing and put them to work on various projects.

they found themselves in even worse circumstances. In 1933, up to 40 percent of African Americans were unemployed. Mexican Americans had trouble finding work when they were passed over for white migratory workers. Both groups experienced the impact of the unspoken rule "last hired, first fired." Despite the efforts of the First Lady, New Deal programs usually maintained the policy of racial segregation, especially in southern states.

Quilting

During the lean times of the 1930s, many women quilted to make use of fabric scraps and to enjoy the creative outlet the activity provided. Wives and mothers had no choice but to mend their families' clothing, since new clothing was not in the family budget. However, clothing that was too worn to fix was cut up and used for quilts.

In 1933, the Chicago World's Fair featured a national quilt competition with $7,500 worth of prizes. Women from around the country responded by entering 24,000 quilts.

Jewish Americans also felt the sting of discrimination. Anti-Semitism, or hostility and bigotry against Jews, was on the rise. In Germany, Adolf Hitler and his Nazi Party blamed Jewish bankers for their country's economic crisis. The popular broadcasts of Detroit, Michigan, priest Charles Coughlin reinforced this bigotry.

Native Americans had one of the lowest life expectancy rates in the nation. The Indian Reorganization Act of 1934 was an element of the New Deal that addressed this group of Americans. The act allowed tribes to organize into corporations that could engage in business. Programs were also established to conserve Native American lands, establish better education and health facilities on reservations, and preserve tribal heritages. All of this was intended to help Native Americans build a strong economic foundation, which was Roosevelt's goal for all Americans and the United States as a whole.

Dorothea Lange's photos of Florence Thompson and her children epitomized the despair of so many Americans during the Depression.

On April 3, 1939, thousands of job seekers waited in line at the navy yard in Charlestown, Massachusetts, for 25 jobs and a place on a work list.

PUTTING AMERICANS BACK TO WORK

One of the biggest and most immediate goals of the Roosevelt administration was to put Americans back to work. Not everyone agreed with the president's programs and projects. President Roosevelt believed it was important to help those millions of Americans who had been out of work for months start earning a paycheck again. Roosevelt and his advisers also believed putting people back to work was better for their morale than simply receiving welfare checks.

INTERNAL STRUGGLE

Two kinds of work relief highlighted the political debate between liberals and conservatives over the legitimacy and cost of the New Deal. Secretary of the Interior Harold Ickes was responsible for the long-range projects of the Public Works Administration (PWA), including the building of roads, schools, bridges, and hospitals. Harry Hopkins dealt with the immediate distribution of emergency funds through the Civil Works Administration (CWA) and the Federal Emergency Relief Act (FERA).

Ickes and Hopkins were stubborn and did not agree on many things. Ickes favored a trickle-down

Praise for the New Deal

Representative Clifton A. Woodrum of Virginia served his state from 1923 to 1945. He spoke well of Roosevelt's New Deal: "You do not have to look far to find many fine things about the relief program . . . Much of a notable character has been accomplished that will remain all through the years . . . every congressman saw that as he went through his district. . . . Why it sounds almost like the accomplishments of King Solomon."[1]

approach to healing the nation's economy. He
believed funding large-scale projects through the
PWA would eventually employ many people and
provide them with income. Hopkins supported the
trickle-up theory. He believed putting money in the
pockets of the poor would allow them to purchase
goods again. This would boost sales and put people
back to work in factories and businesses.

Ickes, along with many conservatives, criticized
the CWA and FERA programs. Ickes argued
that their workers did little more than complete
unimportant tasks, such as raking leaves. He called
this a boondoggle—inefficient and wasteful work.
Unfortunately, the two men found themselves
competing for the same funds, and a feud
developed.

In response to his critics, Roosevelt pointed
to the number of projects built by the PWA and
to the fact that some 4.2 million men had found
employment through the CWA and FERA during the
winter of 1933–1934. This enabled them to afford
rent, heat, food, and clothing for their families.
The program was so successful that Roosevelt secured
even more funding from Congress to continue the
effort under FERA.

Birth of the WPA

As the Depression continued, millions of Americans found at least temporary work through one of Roosevelt's New Deal programs. But unemployment remained a problem. In 1934, nearly 20 percent of the work force remained without permanent jobs. More was needed to correct the economic crisis.

On May 6, 1935, FERA was transformed into a more permanent agency: the Works Progress Administration (WPA). Congress approved $4 billion to fund the WPA and the PWA. Harry Hopkins headed the WPA and he and Ickes fought for funding. Most of the funds would go to the WPA.

Depending on where they lived—city or country—and how skilled they were, WPA workers received anywhere from $19 to $94 a month. In the 1930s, this was enough to support a family. Over eight years, the

Employing Women

The Works Progress Administration employed a fair number of women. Most of them worked on sewing projects. After being taught to use sewing machines, these women made clothing and bedding for orphanages and hospitals. Others worked in children's nurseries and camps, on canning and school lunch projects, and in mattress centers and bird and wildflower sanctuaries.

program put more than 8.5 million people back to work. The WPA was responsible for construction in almost every community—125,000 public buildings, 78,000 bridges, 651,000 miles (1,047,683 km) of roads and streets, 25,000 playgrounds, and 700 miles (1,127 km) of airport runways. Charges of boondoggle continued, but that criticism paled alongside the lives saved and the structures that endured for years thereafter.

WPA Posters

As part of the New Deal's Works Progress Administration, artists were hired to create posters depicting the work of various government-sponsored programs and projects. The bold, brightly colored, modern-looking posters also encouraged people to join in cultural, educational, community, and health programs. Some called for people to "Eat Fruit, Be Healthy," or "Keep Your Teeth Clean." Other posters promoted travel and tourism or WPA-sponsored concerts, plays, and exhibitions—all free to the public.

More than 35,000 different posters were designed, and nearly 2 million were printed. Today, only 2,000 or so of them still exist. The Library of Congress holds the largest collection of posters, approximately 900 in all.

When the United States entered World War II, the artists who designed the WPA posters were put to work creating war posters. Posters with the slogan "Uncle Sam Wants You" called for people to join the military. Other posters warned of the dangers of spies and discussing military information. Still others encouraged Americans to conserve resources such as water for the production of war materials.

Assistance for Students

During the Depression, many young people had been forced to drop out of school. Some had to work at any job they could find to help their families. Others chose not to go to school if it meant wearing worn-out clothing and not having shoes. The National Youth Administration (NYA) was a division of the WPA created to assist students.

In 1935, the NYA began providing grants to high school and college students in exchange for part-time work. Jobs included positions as typists, janitors, library staff, and laboratory workers. The NYA also provided small payments to school-aged children for doing work after school hours. In addition, nearly 200,000 young men and women were put to work on special projects on campus.

Students received from $6 for those in high school to $30 a month for graduate students. While these rates were not high, they allowed many students to remain in school.

Writers, Musicians, and Artists at Work

As part of the Federal Writers' Project, 6,600 writers were employed to teach more than 1 million illiterate Americans to read and write. Similarly, under the Federal Music Project more than 15,000 musicians were put to work performing and teaching school children to play musical instruments. Artists also gave painting, sculpture, and drawing classes to both adults and children. Two well-known participants were Orson Welles and Jackson Pollock.

Recruits in the Works Progress Administration lay a sidewalk in New Jersey in 1938.

The NYA employed 1.5 million high school students, 600,000 college students, and almost 2.7 million unemployed young people between the ages of 16 and 24 who did not attend school.

Help for the Artists

Artists, writers, and musicians were also out of work and needed help. The Federal Writers'

Project originally employed teachers, historians, and writers to create scenic guides to encourage tourism, and then branched out to include more cultural writings. The Federal Art Project paid artists to paint murals and posters for various government uses. The Federal Music Project employed musicians for symphonies, orchestras, and jazz bands as well as provided classes to those in rural and urban areas. The Federal Theater Project put actors and directors back to work. An estimated 1,200 plays were performed all over the country, many in band shells built by the WPA. Tickets were free or very inexpensive, so many Americans in rural areas were able to attend a live play for the first time. When questioned why federal funds were going to artists and musicians, Hopkins fired back, "[T]hey've got to eat just like other people!"[2]

FDR on the NYA

Franklin D. Roosevelt, commonly referred to as FDR, said of the National Youth Administration, "[We] can ill afford to lose the skill and energy of these young men and women. They must have their chance in school, their turn as apprentices and their opportunity for jobs—a chance to work and earn for themselves."[3]

He added:

Under the Federal Art Project, it may interest you to know that we employed professional artists and writers to teach their skills to the youth in rural schools. In Mississippi alone sixty-nine thousand people attended music classes taught by one hundred Federal music teachers.[4]

Despite having their differences, Harry Hopkins and Harold Ickes worked successfully to lead two of the most important programs of the New Deal. The WPA and the PWA both offered short- and long-range relief to millions of Americans.

Muralist Diego Rivera's work served as an inspiration for President Franklin Roosevelt's WPA program.

Harold Ickes, left, turns on the electricity for a farm in Virginia on July 22, 1936, as part of the Rural Electrification Administration.

THE SECOND NEW DEAL

The period from 1935 to 1936 is often referred to as the Second New Deal. Much of the Roosevelt administration's legislation during this time dealt with long-term solutions to the nation's problems. This would be the reform aspect of the New Deal. Programs would address financial assistance for the elderly, taxes, and labor. Upgrading work relief under the Works Progress Administration was an example of this changed focus.

On May 11, 1935, Roosevelt established the Rural Electrification Administration to provide electricity to areas that had never before had that convenience. In August, Congress passed the Public Utility Holding Company Act, which allowed federal agencies to regulate gas and electric companies.

On July 5, the president signed the National Labor Relations Act into law. The law was also known as the Wagner Act, named after New York Senator Robert F. Wagner. It created the National Labor Relations Board to enforce the right of employees to join unions and bargain collectively with management over wages and working conditions. The

"What was the New Deal anyhow? Was it a political plot? Was it just a name for a period in history? Was it a revolution? To all of these questions I answer 'No.' It was something quite different. . . . It was, I think, basically an attitude. An attitude that found voice in expressions like 'the people are what matter to government,' and 'a government should aim to give all the people under its jurisdiction the best possible life.'"[1]

—*Frances Perkins, secretary of Labor and chairperson of the Committee on Economic Security* bill rejuvenated the union movement and led to many strikes that produced higher wages and better working conditions.

SHARE OUR WEALTH PROGRAM

In addition to continuing to try to create jobs for Americans, Roosevelt and his staff were concerned about the poor who were unable or unlikely to find work. Unlike many European nations at the time, the United States had no national social program to deal with the elderly, the unemployed, or the disabled.

Roosevelt was pressured to do something for these people by Louisiana Senator Huey P. Long. Long was advocating the Share Our Wealth program. Long initially supported Roosevelt, but he came to believe the president was not doing enough to end poverty. Long suggested his own program. Many end-poverty schemes had been suggested, but Long's Share Our Wealth program gained popularity, particularly among the poor.

Long believed every American should be guaranteed an annual income of at least $2,000. And he supported the idea of a homestead allowance, which would reward people for owning homes.

Senator Huey Long thought President Roosevelt needed to do more for Americans and proposed the Share Our Wealth program.

Long's plan also included providing free college education to students and pensions for the elderly.

Long's proposed program would be funded by the wealthy, starting at a 1 percent tax on those worth $2 million or more. Individuals earning $8 million or more a year would be taxed at 100 percent. This high level of taxation meant that their income would basically be taken by the government and ideally be distributed to the poor. Long's plan would not become reality. Long was assassinated in 1935. Carl Austin Weiss shot the senator on September 8. Long died two days later.

Social Security Takes Shape

Long and other radicals were unsuccessful in their efforts to redistribute wealth in the United States. However, they did bring attention to poverty and the need to provide permanent aid to people unable to work. There were few pension programs available to most workers. Few laborers and farmers were able to save money for retirement. Most had barely enough income to support themselves and their families while they were working. Those too old to work had to be supported by their families or charities whose funds had been greatly reduced by the Depression. And the problem was growing because Americans were living longer.

"A permanent program for the poor is a poor program."[2]

—*The designers of Social Security*

When Roosevelt took office, he appointed Frances Perkins secretary of the Department of Labor. She was the first female cabinet member in U.S. history. Perkins had been a leader in social reform efforts in New York, where she had improved working conditions in areas such as safety, maximum hours, and wages. In June 1934, Perkins was also appointed chairperson of the president's Committee on Economic Security. The Social Security Act was created while she held this position.

Perkins combined the knowledge of economists, statisticians, and insurance executives to help write a bill to put before Congress. The Social Security Act of 1935 called for providing old-age and survivors insurance. Passage of the bill would mean providing an income to Americans over

Social Security's Controversies

Since it was signed into law on August 14, 1935, the Social Security Act has been amended several times, and it has been the subject of much controversy. Today, one of the biggest topics of concern is that Social Security will not have enough money to pay retirement benefits to the next generation of elderly Americans. This generation, sometimes called the baby-boomers, is huge compared to previous generations. In addition, with the increase in life expectancy, baby-boomers will likely live longer than members of previous generations.

The program has grown to enormous proportions. Social Security struggles with the problem that annual payments to retired Americans in the near future will cost more than payroll deductions and employer contributions. Without government action, the program stands to go bankrupt.

Another ongoing criticism of Social Security has to do with personal responsibility. Some critics believe individuals should save money and invest for retirement on their own, rather than rely on the government to do it for them.

Secretary of Labor Frances Perkins

the age of 65, even after they stopped working. Both employees and employers would contribute to the federal fund through a tax.

The bill also included unemployment insurance, which would provide aid to people who were unemployed and searching for work. These people would receive an income while they looked for work. In a time of great joblessness, a plan for unemployment insurance was vital. The Social Security Act helped states establish systems for offering aid to the unemployed.

The legislation also authorized funding to states to provide for dependent children, the disabled, and public health activities. In addition to helping those greatest in need, another motive for this legislation was that it would put money in the hands of people who would readily spend it. This would help stimulate the ailing economy.

Opposition to Social Security

Conservatives opposed the plan for Social Security. They viewed it as a socialist scheme—one that would give the federal government the power to redistribute income from the wealthy to the poor. Other critics argued that employers would increase prices for goods and services to pay their half of the Social Security tax.

"This law represents a cornerstone in a structure which is being built but is by no means completed—a structure intended to lessen the force of possible future depressions, to act as a protection to future administrations of the Government against the necessity of going deeply into debt to furnish relief to the needy—a law to flatten out the peaks and valleys of deflation and of inflation—in other words, a law that will take care of human needs and at the same time provide for the United States an economic structure of vastly greater soundness."[3]

—*Franklin D. Roosevelt, after signing the Social Security bill into law on August 14, 1935*

First Social Security Payment

The first monthly Social Security payment, check number 00-000-001, was issued to Ida May Fuller of Ludlow, Vermont, on January 31, 1940. Fuller had worked as a legal secretary and paid three years' worth of Social Security taxes before retiring—a sum totaling $24.75. When she passed away at the age of 100, Fuller had collected a total of $22,888.92 in Social Security benefits.

Industrialists insisted that creating such a program would discourage Americans from saving money and being responsible for themselves.

Perkins worried that Congress would not pass the Social Security Act. In fact, the idea behind the bill was revolutionary. If the bill passed, it would be the first federal program of social welfare in U.S. history.

The president signed the Social Security Act into law on August 14, 1935. Within two years, the Social Security Board was collecting money that employers withheld from employees' paychecks. A few years later, the program began paying the first Social Security benefits, initially in lump-sum payments, followed by monthly payments. Critics remained doubtful about the program, but it was working.

A 1936 poster issued by the Social Security Board to promote the application for Social Security cards

*President Roosevelt spoke to a nationwide audience
from the White House on April 28, 1935.*

Too Much Power?

he 1936 presidential election would be a
vote on the New Deal. Many questions were
on voters' minds. They pondered the effectiveness
of the New Deal and whether Americans were better
off than they were four years before. Some thought

perhaps the federal government had gone too far and weakened the free market system. Others questioned President Roosevelt's leadership, wondering if he was a dictator similar to those emerging in Europe.

Many believed he was leading the United States in the wrong direction. They blasted him for assuming too much power over private business. Conservatives strongly opposed the National Recovery Administration, which had threatened their right to determine production levels and prices. Roosevelt's opponents formed the Liberty League to fight the New Deal and accused him of violating the Constitution and ending individual liberties. Business owners blamed him for workers' strikes, which interfered with running their businesses.

In 1936, Roosevelt toured the nation, giving speeches and greeting crowds of Americans who viewed him as the nation's savior. Despite opposition to the New Deal, on November 3, Roosevelt was reelected in a landslide victory over Kansas Governor Alfred M. Landon.

First Houses

Fiorello La Guardia was elected mayor of New York City in 1933. He focused on tearing down some of the city's worst tenements, renovating others, and building new housing. The first new development was First Houses. It was the first low-income housing project ever sponsored by the U.S. government. Getting an apartment in First Houses required proof of insurance, $100 in the bank, and membership in a fraternal society.

Voters also put more Democrats into the U.S. Congress. The only part of the federal government the New Deal administration did not control was the judicial branch.

THE "COURT-PACKING" SCHEME

From 1935 to 1936, the U.S. Supreme Court had heard several cases challenging the constitutionality of New Deal programs. Critics argued that the programs violated the basic ideas set forth in the Constitution. If the Court justices agreed, the programs would be ruled unconstitutional, making them unlawful.

The U.S. Supreme Court

The U.S. Supreme Court is the highest judicial body in the nation. Cases come before the Court after they have been tried in lower-level courts. Thus, decisions in local, state, and district courts can be appealed to a higher court. Each state has its own supreme court, which has the final say in court cases that challenge state law. Only cases that challenge federal law can be tried before the U.S. Supreme Court.

At the time, six of the nine justices felt the government did not have the right to interfere with private business. Many cases were decided in favor of Roosevelt's critics. The Agricultural Adjustment Act and the National Recovery Administration were two major programs struck down by the Court. Several smaller programs were also ruled unconstitutional. Roosevelt worried that more of his legislation would

Members of the U.S. Supreme Court in 1930

be ended by Supreme Court rulings, including the Social Security Act.

The president felt the only way to ensure the safety of his New Deal programs was to change the Court. Supreme Court justices are appointed by the president, and they serve for life. Only when one retires or dies is another appointed. Roosevelt did not think any changes in the existing Court would be made soon. If he could expand the Court, Roosevelt could appoint judges who would be less likely to oppose his New Deal legislation.

On February 5, 1937, Roosevelt presented to Congress a proposal for appointing a new federal judge for each one who had reached the age of 70½ but had not retired. This meant that the term *federal judge* would also apply to U.S. Supreme Court justices.

If the Judiciary Reorganization Bill of 1937 passed, Roosevelt would be able to select up to six new Supreme Court justices. He would surely choose judges who would support his New Deal. This so-called court packing would give Roosevelt control of the judicial branch of the U.S. government.

Roosevelt tried to convince Congress that the current justices were perhaps too old and out of

---

Numerous Critics

President Roosevelt faced numerous criticisms for his New Deal legislation. People disliked his actions for a variety of reasons. Responding to passage of the Wagner Act, business owners blamed Roosevelt and his New Deal for the strikes and the disruption in production that interfered with their businesses. Entrepreneurs believed unions now had too much power.

Others claimed Roosevelt's policies were bringing socialism to the United States. Critics charged that relief programs were undermining the character of the people; it was wrong for the government to give handouts—people should be responsible for supporting themselves and their families. Providing welfare payments was viewed as encouraging people to be irresponsible and lazy. Critics of welfare argued that charities and religious organizations were available to help people in need.

On the other hand, some people criticized Roosevelt for not doing enough for Americans. Norman Thomas was the Socialist Party's candidate for president in 1932. He accused the president of selling out to the business elite and not doing enough to help the working class. And elected officials such as Huey Long had challenged Roosevelt to do more for the poor.

touch to do their jobs well. He wanted to "bring to the decision of social and economic problems younger men who have had personal experience and contact with modern facts and circumstances under which average men have to live and work."[1]

Many Americans were angry with Roosevelt for trying to change the system of government established by the nation's founders. The president was accused of trying to do away with the U.S. Constitution, though it says nothing about the number of justices required for the Court. Even Vice President Garner was disgusted with Roosevelt's plan to change the U.S. government.

Although Roosevelt fought hard for the bill, Congress rejected it. However, ironically, in the midst of the great court-packing debate, the Supreme Court justices became more accepting of New Deal legislation. Social Security and the Wagner Act were approved. And over the remainder of his presidency, Roosevelt appointed eight new justices to the Supreme Court.

"If by that phrase 'packing the Court' it is charged that I wish to place on the bench spineless puppets who would disregard the law and would decide specific cases as I wished them to be decided, I make this answer: that no President fit for his office would appoint, and no Senate of honorable men fit for their office would confirm, that kind of appointees to the Supreme Court."[2]

—*Franklin D. Roosevelt in a fireside chat*

The Fair Labor Standards Act

The Fair Labor Standards Act is still in effect today and has undergone many changes since it was passed in 1938. It has been updated several times to increase the minimum wage and to shorten the workweek to 40 hours. The Equal Pay Act of 1963 amended the law, making it illegal to pay workers lower wages based on gender. Men and women must be paid the same wage for the same work. Other changes include protecting volunteer time for employees and the jobs of employees who require a medical leave from work.

RECESSION

The year 1937 was a hard one for Roosevelt. He had cut spending to balance the budget, and the economy had nearly collapsed. By May 1938, the jobless rate had risen from 7 million to nearly 11 million. Republicans blamed the president for the "Roosevelt Recession."

Roosevelt attempted to spur the economy. Additional funds were made available to the Works Progress Administration, and more public housing projects were approved. On June 25, 1938, Roosevelt pushed through the last of his major reform laws. The Fair Labor Standards Act created a 44-hour workweek, time-and-a-half wages for overtime, and a minimum hourly wage of 25¢. It also banned child labor and restricted the jobs minors could hold. Roosevelt continued to work to help his nation and his people survive and thrive.

A cartoon about the court-packing plan shows justices looking like Roosevelt because they would likely share his beliefs.

The Nazis' invasion of Poland in September 1939 started World War II.

WAR AIDS RECOVERY

After taking office in 1932, Roosevelt and his administration presented Americans with a range of programs to help them recover from the Great Depression. Between early 1933 and late 1937, New Deal programs had put millions of Americans back to work, but in 1940, millions more were still without jobs. The economic downturn of 1937, called by some the "Roosevelt Recession," had all but undone the efforts of the New Deal. Despite Roosevelt's efforts, the New Deal failed to lead the United States out of the Depression. World War II would provide the solution to the nation's economic crisis.

WORLD WAR II

The Great Depression was a worldwide crisis. Germany had begun economic recovery by massive spending on military rearmament. Adolf Hitler's Nazi government gained power, while the rest of Europe struggled with high unemployment and poverty. Before long, Europe would be forced to deal with this fact.

During this time of global economic crisis, Japan, Germany, and Italy all tried to improve their economies through military conquests. Japan had invaded China in 1931. And Hitler was planning to attack neighboring countries. By 1939, Europe was on the verge of war.

On September 1, 1939, Germany invaded Poland. In response, Great Britain and France

declared war against Germany.
In June 1940, France fell to the
Nazis, and Italy entered the war as
Germany's ally. When Germany
invaded the Soviet Union in June
1941, that country joined forces with
Great Britain and France against the
fascist powers.

The United States decided not
to get involved in the war. After the
losses the United States had sustained
during World War I, Americans
were not eager to enter another
war. Congress passed neutrality
legislation during the 1930s to
avoid another war.

Remaining Neutral

On September 3, 1939,
after Roosevelt heard that
Germany had bombed
Great Britain, he reassured
Americans with these
words: "This nation will
remain a neutral nation,
but I cannot ask that every
American remain neutral
in thought as well. . . . I
hope the United States
will keep out of this war.
I believe that it will. And
I give you assurance and
reassurance that every
effort of your government
will be directed toward
that end."[1]

Responding to the War

Roosevelt went along with the mood in the
nation, but by 1937, he realized the United
States could no longer ignore its international
responsibilities. He began to build up the army
and the navy. He also pressured Japan to end its
war in China. When the war broke out in Europe,
Roosevelt took steps to assist Great Britain.

In June 1940, the U.S. War Department released outdated and surplus stocks of arms and planes to the British. On September 3, Roosevelt arranged to transfer 50 aged destroyers to the British in exchange for leases on British bases located in the Caribbean. By using this exchange method, Roosevelt kept the United States from being directly involved in the war but was able to provide aid to U.S. ally Great Britain, who was under heavy assault by Nazi Germany.

In September, Congress authorized a draft—the first peacetime compulsory military service in U.S. history. In November, Roosevelt ran for reelection. He beat Republican candidate Wendell Willkie, making history as the first U.S. president elected to serve three terms.

On March 11, 1941, Congress passed the Lend-Lease Act, which allowed the United States to ship weapons to friendly governments in exchange for payment at a later date. Millions of dollars were now being spent on ships and planes. Producing these items and other war supplies created numerous jobs. Americans rushed back to work, assisting with the war effort. After ten long years, the Great Depression was finally over.

The battleship USS Arizona *toppled into the sea during a Japanese surprise attack on Pearl Harbor, Hawaii, on December 7, 1941. The assault forced the United States out of its isolationism and into the war.*

INTO THE WAR

On December 7, 1941, Japanese fighter planes bombed the U.S. naval base at Pearl Harbor, Hawaii. Congress declared war on Japan the next day. Hitler declared war on the United States, which did the same in return. The United States was now an official member of the Allied forces.

The nation had an immediate need for arms and weapons. U.S. factories began working at full capacity. With men being drafted to fight in the war, women were hired to do factory work that used to be done solely by men, such as welding, drilling, and riveting. The U.S. military also employed 350,000 women as typists, nurses, mail sorters, clerks, and even pilots in civil air squadrons. Unemployment dropped dramatically. By 1944, the rate hit an all-time low of 1.2 percent.

World War II raged until 1945. Germany surrendered in early May, but Japan did not officially surrender until September, after the United States dropped two atomic bombs on the Japanese cities of Hiroshima and Nagasaki. Perhaps as many as 60 million people died in the war, including approximately 400,000 Americans. For the United States, the war was costly, but it ended the Great Depression.

"Yesterday, December 7, 1941—a date which will live in infamy—the United States of America was suddenly and deliberately attacked by naval and air forces of the Empire of Japan. . . . With confidence in our armed forces—with the unbounding determination of our People—we will gain the inevitable triumph—so help us God. I ask that the Congress declare that since the unprovoked and dastardly attack by Japan on Sunday, December 7th, 1941, a state of War has existed between the United States and the Japanese Empire."[2]

—*Franklin D. Roosevelt, speech to Congress, December 8, 1941*

ENDURING CHANGES

Roosevelt's administration had forever changed the role of government in the United States. Gone were the days when the economy was left to fluctuate on its own. When Roosevelt became president in 1933, government spending was about $5 billion. By 1934, New Deal programs had increased spending to $6.6 billion. By 1936, the figure had risen to $8.4 billion. Still, New Deal spending was nowhere near the amount the government paid during World War II, when federal spending totaled almost $320 billion.

Critics of the New Deal were quick to point out that World

Rosie the Riveter

During World War II, thousands of women went to work in factories, taking over jobs once done by men. Many of these women were encouraged to take jobs by a fictional character named Rosie the Riveter, who was created as part of an advertising campaign to recruit women workers for the war effort.

A real-life "Rosie" was usually dressed in overalls and used tools such as drills and welding torches. For her work, she was paid approximately $30 a week—about half the $55 paid to a man doing the same job.

Katie Grant worked as a "Rosie" in a shipyard in California:

I worked the graveyard shift 12:00–8:00 a.m., in the shipyard. I took classes on how to weld. I had leather gloves, leather pants, big hood, goggles and a leather jacket. . . .

They put me forty feet down in the bottom of the ship to be a tacker. I filled the long seams of the cracks in the ship corners full of hot lead and then brushed them good and you could see how pretty it was. . . .

Lots of people came to Richmond to work in the shipyards. Lots of women went to work to help with the war. I told [my husband] later that I helped to make a ship for him to come home in.[3]

War II put Americans back to work and ended the Depression. However, New Deal programs did uphold democracy. European countries such as Germany, Italy, and Russia fell under the control of dictators, who robbed citizens of their rights. In contrast, the United States endured and became stronger and better.

The New Deal had other lasting effects. Programs such as the Works Progress Administration and the Public Works Administration produced schools, hospitals, parks, roads, and other structures that still exist. The Civilian Conservation Corps's work on national and state parks has also lasted.

The New Deal helped protect workers by creating standards for hours worked and minimum wages paid—standards still enforced. New Deal programs also made child labor illegal and provided a range of benefits to U.S. workers.

Perhaps the best-known program of Roosevelt's administration, Social Security, also remains in effect. It has provided financial security for millions of retired citizens and

"What doesn't show up on the performance indicators was the restoration of hope, and I think that's immeasurable, and . . . America today might be a quite different country if Roosevelt had not managed to restore America's belief in itself."[4]

—Verne Newton, director of the FDR Library, 1991–1998

unemployment benefits to millions more workers in search of jobs.

Not all of Roosevelt's New Deal programs were successful. Some did not work as the president and his administration had hoped they would, and others provided only temporary solutions to long-term problems. Some programs were declared unconstitutional and struck down by the U.S. Supreme Court.

During the Great Depression, the United States had a president who was willing to try a variety of ideas to help solve the economic crisis. Roosevelt surrounded himself with creative, intelligent advisers who offered a variety of opinions. He hired passionate people to head his programs who were dedicated to one goal: saving and securing the American people.

Roosevelt's New Deal forever changed the U.S. economy, government, and society. Its programs offered immediate help to the poor and unemployed and shaped the nature of work for generations to come. But perhaps most importantly, Franklin Delano Roosevelt's New Deal boosted the morale of the American people and restored their faith in the future of the country.

Conrad Albrizio created a mural fresco depicting phases of Roosevelt's New Deal, which he dedicated to the president on January 24, 1935.

TIMELINE

1929

The U.S. stock market crashes on October 24.

1933

Roosevelt is inaugurated as president of the United States on March 4.

1933

Banks close on March 6 for a national bank holiday, the first of many steps to save and restore the U.S. economy.

1933

On March 31, Roosevelt signs the Civilian Conservation Corps Reforestation Relief Act into law.

1933

On May 12, Congress passes the Federal Emergency Relief Act (FERA).

1933

On May 13, Congress passes the Agricultural Adjustment Act.

1933

On March 9, the U.S. Congress passes the Emergency Banking Act.

1933

On March 12, Roosevelt gives his first fireside chat on the radio.

1933

On March 13, banks are allowed to reopen.

1933

On May 18, the Tennessee Valley Authority is established to build dams and provide cheap electrical power.

1933

On June 13, the Home Owners' Loan Corporation is created.

1933

On June 16, Congress creates the Public Works Administration and the National Recovery Administration.

TIMELINE

1933

On November 8, the Civil Works Administration is created to fund state-level construction projects to employ workers immediately.

1935

The Resettlement Administration is created on April 30.

1935

On May 6, Congress passes a bill transforming FERA into the more permanent Works Progress Administration.

1936

Roosevelt is reelected as president on November 3.

1938

Roosevelt signs the Fair Labor Standards Act on June 25.

1939

Led by Adolf Hitler, Germany invades Poland on September 1, starting World War II.

1935

1935

1935

On May 11, the Rural Electrification Administration is created to bring electricity to more Americans.

On July 5, Roosevelt signs the National Labor Relations Act.

The president signs the Social Security Act into law on August 14.

1940

1941

1941

Roosevelt wins a third presidential election; he is the first and only individual to ever do so.

On March 11, Congress approves the Lend-Lease Act, providing Great Britain with war materials without immediate payment.

On December 8, the United States declares war on Japan and enters World War II; recovery from the Great Depression follows quickly.

Essential Facts

Date of Event

October 24, 1929–December 8, 1941

Place of Event

United States of America

Key Players

- ❖ Franklin D. Roosevelt
- ❖ Eleanor Roosevelt
- ❖ U.S. Congress
- ❖ The American people
- ❖ Harry Hopkins
- ❖ Frances Perkins
- ❖ Harold Ickes
- ❖ Adolf Hitler
- ❖ Great Britain
- ❖ Japan

HIGHLIGHTS OF EVENT

❖ Following the stock market crash on October 24, 1929, the U.S. economy slumped, as did economies worldwide.

❖ New York Governor Franklin D. Roosevelt ran for president in 1932 on a platform of a New Deal that would turn around the U.S. economy.

❖ Franklin D. Roosevelt won the election, was sworn in as president of the United States on March 4, 1933, and took the first step in his New Deal on March 5.

❖ During his first 100 days in office, Roosevelt passed a record-breaking number of laws to help the country recover from the Great Depression.

❖ After Japanese fighters bombed the U.S. naval base at Pearl Harbor, Hawaii, the United States entered World War II on December 8, 1941.

❖ Entry into the war sent men overseas, which brought women to factory positions that included work such as welding, drilling, and riveting. In addition, the U.S. military employed 350,000 women as typists, nurses, mail sorters, clerks, and even pilots in civil air squadrons.

❖ World War II brought financial recovery to the United States. Unemployment dropped dramatically. By 1944, the unemployment rate was at an all-time low of only 1.2 percent.

QUOTE

"This great Nation will endure as it has endured, will revive and will prosper. So, first of all, let me assert my firm belief that the only thing we have to fear is fear itself—nameless, unreasoning, unjustified terror which paralyzes needed efforts to convert retreat into advance."—*Franklin D. Roosevelt*

ADDITIONAL RESOURCES

SELECT BIBLIOGRAPHY

Freidel, Frank. *Franklin D. Roosevelt: Launching the New Deal*. Boston: Little, Brown, 1973.

Himmelberg, Robert F. *The Great Depression and the New Deal*. Westport, CT: Greenwood, 2001.

Schlesinger, Arthur Meier. *The New Deal in Action, 1933–1939*. New York: Macmillan, 1940.

Schwarz, Jordan A. *The New Dealers: Power Politics in the Age of Roosevelt*. New York: Knopf, 1993.

Taylor, Nick. *American-Made: The Enduring Legacy of the WPA: When FDR Put the Nation to Work*. New York: Bantam Dell, 2008.

FURTHER READING

Badger, Anthony. *The New Deal: The Depression Years, 1933–1940*. New York: Hill and Wang, 1989.

Collier, Christopher, and James Lincoln Collier. *Progressivism, the Great Depression, and the New Deal*. New York: Benchmark, 2001.

Heinemann, Ronald L. *Depression and New Deal in Virginia: The Enduring Dominion*. Charlottesville, VA: University of Virginia Press, 1983.

Lawson, Don. *FDR's New Deal*. New York: Crowell, 1979.

Leuchtenburg, William E. *The FDR Years: On Roosevelt and his Legacy*. New York: Columbia UP, 1995.

Schraff, Anne E. *The Great Depression and the New Deal: America's Economic Collapse and Recovery*. New York: Franklin Watts, 1990.

Web Links

To learn more about Franklin Delano Roosevelt and his New Deal, visit ABDO Publishing Company online at **www.abdopublishing.com**. Web sites about Roosevelt and his New Deal are featured on our Book Links page. These links are routinely monitored and updated to provide the most current information available.

Places To Visit

Franklin Delano Roosevelt Memorial
West Basin Drive, along Cherry Tree Walk, the western edge of the Tidal Basin near the National Mall, Washington, DC
202-426-6841
www.nps.gov/fdrm
The memorial honors the president, the First Lady, and the men and women of the Great Depression era. It includes a sculpture of men in a breadline and a statue of Roosevelt seated in a wheelchair.

Franklin D. Roosevelt Presidential Library and Museum
4079 Albany Post Road, Hyde Park, NY 12538
800-FDR-VISIT (337-84748), 845-486-7770
www.fdrlibrary.marist.edu
The museum is the nation's first presidential library. It houses and preserves 18,000 cubic feet of manuscripts, letters, audiovisual materials, photographs, and nearly 30,000 objects related to Franklin and Eleanor Roosevelt.

Rosie the Riveter/World War II Home Front National Historical Park
1401 Marina Way South, Richmond, CA 94804
510-232-5050
www.nps.gov/rori
The park preserves the stories of those Americans who worked on the home front to support the country during World War II. Visitors can tour the USS *Red Oak Victory*, the last remaining ship made in the shipyards of Richmond.

Glossary

administration
> The group of people who work for a president; also a president's term in office.

bankrupt
> Financially ruined.

conservative
> A political view based on caution and moderation.

crisis
> An emergency or a disaster.

despair
> A feeling of hopelessness.

destitute
> Suffering from extreme poverty.

devastation
> A situation of great damage and waste.

economic
> Related to producing, selling, and consuming goods and services.

foreclosure
> The legal process by which a bank takes back a house, a farm, or other property because its owner has not made the payments on the home loan from the bank.

grant
> A gift of money; money given that does not need to be repaid.

inaugural
> Related to the official act of putting someone in office, such as the president.

incumbent
> Someone who holds a specific office or position.

legislation
> An act or a law or a group of related acts or laws.

liberal
> Unrestricted by policy or tradition; broad-minded and freethinking.

morale
> Someone's sense of well-being or confidence.

mortgage
> A loan taken out from a bank or other lending institution to buy a house, a farm, or other property.

pension
> A retirement fund that is paid out to an individual in regular amounts, such as monthly.

ratified
> Formally approved or confirmed.

recession
> A decrease in or slowing of economic activity.

stock
> A share of a publicly held company or the total shares issued by a company.

unconstitutional
> Against or inconsistent with the basic ideas set forth in the U.S. Constitution.

welfare
> Assistance given to those in need, often in the form of money and food.

Source Notes

Chapter 1. A New President
1. "Books: A President's Ordeal." *Time.com*. 8 Sept. 1952.
24 Oct. 2009 <http://www.time.com/time/magazine/
article/0,9171,935714,00.html>.
2. Frank Freidel. *Franklin D. Roosevelt: Launching the New Deal*. Boston,
MA: Little, Brown, 1973. 4–5.
3. "Roosevelt, Franklin D." *Encyclopaedia Britannica Online Library
Edition*. 2009. 24 Oct. 2009 <http://www.library.eb.com/eb/
article-23942>.

Chapter 2. The Roaring Twenties
1. Evelyn Hawkins, Fran Stancavage, Julia Mitchell, Madeline
Goodman, and Stephen Lazer. *Learning About Our World and Our Past:
Using the Tools and Resources of Geography and U.S. History: A Report of the 1994
Assessment*. Washington, DC: U.S. Department of Education Office
of Educational Research and Improvement, 1998. 42.

Chapter 3. Roosevelt Takes Action
1. Nick Taylor. *American-Made: The Enduring Legacy of the WPA: When FDR
Put the Nation to Work*. New York: Bantam Dell, 2008. 1.
2. "Surviving the Dust Bowl." *American Experience*. PBS.org.
22 Jan. 2009. 25 Oct. 2009 <http://www.pbs.org/wgbh/
americanexperience/dustbowl/introduction>.
3. "Teaching With Documents: FDR's First Inaugural Address."
TheNationalArchives.gov. 24 Oct 2009 <http://www.archives.gov/
education/lessons/fdr-inaugural/>.

Chapter 4. The New Deal
1. Michael Waldman. *My Fellow Americans: The Most Important Speeches
of America's Presidents, from George Washington to George W. Bush, Volume 2*.
Naperville, IL: Sourcebooks, 2003. 95.
2. "FDR in his first Fireside Chat about the banking crisis in
1933." *C-SPAN.org*. 2009. 8 Dec. 2009 <http://whitehouse.c-span.
org/Video/ByPresident/FDRs-Fireside-Chat.aspx>.

3. Otto Friedrich, Hays Gorey, and Ruth Mehrtens
Galvin. "F.D.R.'s Disputed Legend." *Time.com*. 1 Feb. 1982.
25 Oct. 2009 <http://www.time.com/time/magazine/
article/0,9171,954983-6,00.html>.

Chapter 5. Getting Back on Track
1. "'I Remember . . .'—Reminiscences of the Great Depression."
Michigan.gov. 2009. 24 Oct. 2009 <http://www.michigan.gov/
hal/0,1607,7-160-17451_18670_18793-53511--,00.html>.
2. Cabell Phillips. *From the Crash to the Blitz*. New York: Fordham UP,
2000. 232.

Chapter 6. Relief, Recovery, and Reform
1. Kenneth T. Walsh. "The First 100 Days: Franklin Roosevelt
Pioneered the 100-Day Concept." *USNews.com*. 12 Feb.
2009. 25 Oct. 2009 <http://www.usnews.com/articles/news/
history/2009/02/12/the-first-100-days-franklin-roosevelt-
pioneered-the-100-day-concept.html>.
2. Library of Congress. "Dorothea Lange's 'Migrant Mother'
Photographs in the Farm Security Administration Collection: An
Overview." *Prints & Photographs Reading Room Online*. 4 Apr. 2009. 8
Dec. 2009 <http://www.loc.gov/rr/print/list/128_migm.html>.

Chapter 7. Putting Americans Back to Work
1. R. L. Heinemann. *Depression and New Deal in Virginia: The Enduring
Dominion*. Charlottesville, VA: UP of Virginia, 1983. 103.
2. D. M. Foy. *No Time for Glory: The Story of a Dismissed Legend*.
Bloomington, IN: AuthorHouse, 2004. 13.
3. H. Watkins. *The Hungry Years: A Narrative History of the Great Depression in
America*. New York: Holt, 1999. 269.
4. D. M. Foy. *No Time for Glory: The Story of a Dismissed Legend*.
Bloomington, IN: AuthorHouse, 2004. 13.

SOURCE NOTES CONTINUED

Chapter 8. The Second New Deal
1. "Social Security Pioneers: Frances Perkins." *SSA.gov*. 25 Oct. 2009 <http://www.ssa.gov/history/fpbiossa.html>.
2. "SSA History." *SSA.gov*. 25 Oct. 2009 <http://www.ssa.gov/history/fdrstate.html>.
3. Martha Derthick. *Policymaking for Social Security*. Washington, DC: Brookings Institute. 217.

Chapter 9. Too Much Power?
1. Kermit Hall and John J. Patrick. *The Pursuit of Justice: Supreme Court Decisions that Shaped America*. New York: Oxford UP, 2006. 94.
2. "Fireside Chat on Reorganization of the Judiciary." *Franklin D. Roosevelt Presidential Library and Museum online*. 20 Sept. 2009. 25 Oct. 2009 <http://docs.fdrlibrary.marist.edu/030937.html>.

Chapter 10. War Aids Recovery
1. David C. Taylor. *FDR: A Presidency Revealed*. DVD. Team Productions/History Channel, 2005.
2. "FDR Pearl Harbor Day of Infamy Speech to Congress December 8 1941." *Pearl Harbor.org*. 2009. 25 Oct. 2009 <http://www.pearlharbor.org/speech-fdr-infamy-1941.asp>.
3. Katie Grant. "Wartime Memories." *Rosie the Riveter/WWII Home Front National Historical Park Online*. 25 Oct. 2009 <http://www.rosietheriveter.org/memory.htm>.
4. David C. Taylor. *FDR: A Presidency Revealed*. DVD. Team Productions/History Channel, 2005.

INDEX

ABOUT THE AUTHOR

Susan E. Hamen is a full-time author and editor who finds writing and editing children's books her most rewarding career experiences. She has written educational books on a variety of topics, including the Wright brothers, the Lewis and Clark expedition, and Pearl Harbor. Hamen delights in living immersed in the changing seasons of her home state, Minnesota, along with her husband and two young children. In her spare time, she can usually be found reading, canning, sewing, or working on perfecting her apple pie crust.

PHOTO CREDITS

AP Images, cover, 3, 6, 10, 13, 20, 23, 24, 27, 28, 33, 34, 38, 41, 42, 49, 50, 53, 58, 64, 67, 68, 74, 77, 78, 81, 85, 86, 90, 96 (top), 96 (bottom), 97, 98 (bottom), 99; Ford Motor Co./AP Images, 14; Dorothea Lange/AP Images, 57, 98 (top); WX/AP Images, 71; AP Images, 95